1/2000

TOP 10 HOCKEY GOALIES

Dean Spiros

SPORTS TOP 10

Enslow Publishers, Inc.

44 Fadem Road   PO Box 38
Box 699   Aldershot
Springfield, NJ 07081 Hants GU12 6BP
USA   UK

Library of Congress Cataloging-in-Publication Data

Spiros, Dean.
    Top 10 hockey goalies / Dean Spiros.
        p. cm. — (Sports top 10)
    Includes bibliographical references (p. 46) and index.
    Summary: Profiles the lives and careers of Eddie Belfour, Tony Esposito,
Terry Sawchuk, and seven other legendary hockey goalies.
    ISBN 0-7660-1010-4
    1. Hockey goalkeepers—Biography—Juvenile literature. 2. Hockey goal-
keepers—Rating of—Juvenile literature. [1. Hockey players.] I. Title. II. Series.
GV848.5.A1S75 1998
796.96'2'27'0922—dc21
[B]   97-20168
                                                                    CIP
                                                                    AC

Printed in the United States of America

10 9 8 7 6 5 4 3 2 1

Illustration Credits: Brian Babineau/Hockey Hall of Fame, p. 7; Doug
MacLellan/Hockey Hall of Fame, pp. 9, 10, 13, 25, 34, 37; Frank Prazac/
Hockey Hall of Fame, pp. 14, 17, 19, 21, 31, 38; Graphic Artists/ Hockey Hall
of Fame, pp. 26, 29, 41; Imperial Oil-Turofsky/Hockey Hall of Fame, p. 33;
London Life-Portnoy/Hockey Hall of Fame, pp. 43, 45; Miles Nadal/Hockey
Hall of Fame, p. 23.

Cover Illustration: Dave Sandford/Hockey Hall of Fame

Interior Design: Richard Stalzer

CONTENTS

INTRODUCTION

THE JOB DESCRIPTION WOULD PROBABLY scare away a lot of people: Put on forty pounds of equipment, but be able to move as quick as a cat. Go onto the ice and stand in front of a net like a target. Five large men on skates, carrying sticks, shoot pucks at you from 80 to 100 miles per hour.

But as it has been said for over fifty years, goaltenders are different. They accept the challenge. Those who have emerged as the best in their profession have written hockey history.

Former New York Rangers coach Muzz Patrick talked years ago about how different goaltenders are. "They even play a different game than everyone else," Patrick said. "The closest approach in another sport might be the catcher in baseball. But still, he does things that are baseball—goes up to hit, chases fouls, and so on. In hockey, a goalie does nothing that other players do. Except for his sweater, he even dresses differently, right down to his skates."[1]

Said Boston Bruins general manager Harry Sinden, "Goaltending is to hockey like putting is to golf. It really has no relationship to the rest of the game."[2]

Still, a case could be made for the goaltender's being the most important player on the team. One save can turn around a game. The same can be said if a goaltender lets in a "bad goal." Quick reflexes, confidence, a competitive nature, and concentration are all needed for someone to be successful as a goaltender. The right combination remains a mystery.

"Good goalies come in many shapes, sizes, and styles," Hall of Fame goaltender Ken Dryden said. "So do bad goalies."[3]

Teams do not hesitate to use a No. 1 draft choice on a goaltender if he appears to have "all the tools." But there is a long list of can't-miss prospects who didn't play up to expectations. The best in the game have had one thing in common: They have never stopped working and trying to get better. Hockey's greatest goaltenders weren't all great athletes. They didn't all play with a style that they would recommend to others. But they got the job done.

"If you can stop the puck," said Francois Allaire, long-time goaltending coach of the Montreal Canadiens, "all the other problems disappear."[4]

CAREER STATISTICS

Player	Seasons	Games	Wins	Losses	Ties	Shutouts	GAA*
ED BELFOUR	9	428	204	147	56	31	2.68
MARTIN BRODEUR	5	235	119	67	39	22	2.25
KEN DRYDEN	8	397	258	57	74	46	2.24
TONY ESPOSITO	16	886	423	307	151	76	2.92
GRANT FUHR	16	747	353	250	98	20	3.48
GLENN HALL	18	906	407	327	165	84	2.51
JACQUES PLANTE	18	837	434	246	137	82	2.38
PATRICK ROY	13	652	349	205	74	37	2.72
TERRY SAWCHUK	21	971	435	337	188	103	2.52
BILLY SMITH	18	680	305	233	105	22	3.17

*GAA=Goals Against Average
**Statistics through 1996–97 season.

Ed Belfour

For Most Of The Past Thirty Years, the Chicago Blackhawks have been able to count on their goaltender to anchor the team. In the 1960s, Hall of Famer Glenn Hall was the man. In the 1970s, Tony Esposito took over the reins.

There came a time in the 1980s, however, when the Blackhawks found themselves in the unusual position of needing help in goal. They addressed the problem on the day of the 1987 NHL draft. The Blackhawks signed free-agent goaltender Bob Mason, drafted Jimmy Waite with their No. 1 pick, and added college free agent Ed Belfour from the University of North Dakota.

As things worked out, Mason didn't play well in Chicago and was soon traded. Waite still is trying to establish himself as an NHL goaltender. But Belfour developed into one of the greatest goaltenders in Blackhawks history.

After two seasons in the minor leagues, Belfour became the Blackhawks' No. 1 goaltender. For the next six seasons, chants of "ED-DIE, ED-DIE" came to be the norm at Chicago Stadium, and later the United Center, as Blackhawks fans saluted another standout save by Belfour.

Belfour, who has always claimed he needs to play a lot of games to stay sharp, had a perfect match with coach Mike Keenan. Keenan likes to stay with one hot goaltender, and Belfour was that in 1990–91, his rookie season. Belfour played in 74 games, winning a team record 43. He finished with a 2.47 goals-against average and won the Calder Trophy as the NHL's Rookie of the Year. He also won the Vezina Trophy as the league's top goaltender, as well as the Jennings Trophy for allowing the fewest goals.

Ed Belfour gets himself in a position to make the save. Belfour has won two Vezina Trophies as the league's top goalie.

The Blackhawks and Belfour reached the Stanley Cup Finals in 1992. Belfour established an NHL record by winning 11 straight playoff games. After beating St. Louis in the opening round of the playoffs, the Blackhawks swept Detroit in the Division finals, and Edmonton in the Conference finals. Their dream of their first Stanley Cup championship since 1961 ended when they were swept by Pittsburgh in the Finals.

Belfour is known as an overachiever, a player who has enjoyed success because of his dedication. He doesn't have a classic goaltender's style, but Belfour feels that he hasn't always been given enough credit for what he has accomplished.

"The more people watch me the more they respect me," Belfour said. "If people only watch me once in a while they may not get the full picture."[1]

His career accomplishments include four appearances in the NHL All-Star Game. Only Glenn Hall and Tony Esposito rank ahead of Belfour in career wins as a Blackhawk.

Belfour is one of the best-conditioned players in the NHL. During the off-season, he trains and competes in triathlons, which combine long-distance running with cycling and swimming.

Belfour's Blackhawks career ended on January 25, 1997, when he was traded to the San Jose Sharks. After finishing the 1996–97 season in San Jose, Belfour signed with the Dallas Stars as a free agent.

Belfour left Chicago with only one regret. He was sorry he wasn't able to help win a Stanley Cup for the Blackhawks fans who had given him so much support.

ED BELFOUR

BORN: April 21, 1965, Carman, Manitoba, Canada.

PRO: Chicago Blackhawks, 1988–1996; San Jose Sharks, 1996–1997; Dallas Stars, 1997– .

COLLEGE: University of North Dakota.

RECORDS: Won 11 straight playoff games in 1992, an NHL record since tied by Tom Barrasso and Patrick Roy.

HONORS: Calder Trophy, 1991; Vezina Trophy, 1991, 1993.

Belfour was selected to three All-Star teams as a member of the Chicago Blackhawks. Belfour represented the Dallas Stars in the 1997–98 All-Star Game.

MARTIN BRODEU

Intensely watching the action, Martin Brodeur covers his net.

MARTIN BRODEUR'S BACKGROUND SUGGESTS that being a goaltender was in his blood. Brodeur would like to agree. Brodeur's father, Denis, was a top amateur goaltender in Quebec. He was a member of the 1972 Canadian Olympic team that won a bronze medal. Denis Brodeur then went on to a career as a sports photographer. He spent many nights in the Montreal Forum, taking pictures during Canadiens games. But he never pushed Martin toward being a goaltender, or toward being a hockey player at all.

Martin Brodeur first put on a pair of goalie pads at the age of three. Once he got a taste of what it was like to be in goal, he was hooked.

Martin wasn't the only member of the family to benefit from Denis Brodeur's sports background. Martin's brother, Claude, pitched for five years in the minor-league system of the Montreal Expos.

Brodeur was fourteen when Montreal goaltender Patrick Roy won the Conn Smythe Trophy as the playoffs' Most Valuable Player. Brodeur decided at that moment he would try to copy Roy's style in hopes of one day making it to the NHL.

Brodeur made a name for himself playing junior hockey in Quebec. Then, he was selected in the first round of the 1990 draft by the New Jersey Devils. The Devils made a deal with Calgary to move up to the twentieth pick to select Brodeur. The Devils needed help in goal right away, and Brodeur delivered. Brodeur was only nineteen years old when he made his NHL debut in 1992. He took over as the Devils' No. 1 goaltender in 1993.

Brodeur's first full NHL season was a complete success. He finished 27–11–8 with a goals-against average of 2.40. He was awarded the Calder Trophy as the NHL Rookie of the Year.

New Jersey coach Jacques Lemaire had a great career as a forward with the Montreal Canadiens. He watched as Ken Dryden and Roy helped the Canadiens win the Stanley Cup in their rookie seasons. He saw how confident Brodeur was in goal and decided he could handle the pressure too.

"You try to put the kid in when the team is playing at its best so you don't destroy that confidence," Lemaire said. "They aren't afraid, these young guys."[1]

Brodeur proved it in the 1995 playoffs, his second season with the Devils. He played all sixteen games as New Jersey beat Boston, Pittsburgh, and Philadelphia to reach the Stanley Cup Finals for the first time in team history. But Brodeur saved his best work for the Detroit Red Wings in the Finals. Brodeur allowed only 7 goals in four games as the Devils swept their way to the championship.

Brodeur is an athlete who puts in a lot of time in order to make himself a better player. He's always one of the first players on the ice at the start of practice and one of the last to leave when practice is over. Brodeur has never looked at being a goaltender as being a job. He loves everything about being a professional hockey player.

"Even if a goalie doesn't have a great game he can make the big save that could make the difference between winning and losing," Brodeur said. "I like making the difference."[2]

MARTIN BRODEUR

BORN: May 6, 1972, Montreal, Quebec, Canada.

PRO: New Jersey Devils, 1991– .

RECORDS: Played 4,433 minutes in 1995–1996 season, an NHL
    record.

HONORS: Calder Trophy, 1994; Jennings Trophy, 1996, 1997.

Brodeur and his Devils' teammates celebrate the franchise's first-
ever Stanley Cup victory.

KEN DRYDEN

Ken Dryden strikes his trademark pose during a break in the action. An imposing figure, Dryden was one of the largest goalies in the NHL.

KEN DRYDEN

NO GOALTENDER HAS ACCOMPLISHED MORE in as short a time as Ken Dryden. The Montreal Canadiens great, and Hall of Famer, is remembered as someone who always seemed to be in control.

His trademark was the way he leaned on his stick during a stop in the action. With the knob of his stick tucked under his chin and the toe of the stick aimed down at the ice, Dryden looked like a man in control. And no matter what he faced, he usually was.

At six-feet four-inches and 205 pounds, Dryden was one of the largest goaltenders in the NHL. Boston Bruins center Phil Esposito once said facing Dryden was like shooting at an octopus.

Dryden grew up in Islington, a suburb of Toronto. The Drydens' backyard included a long paved stretch. It proved to be a perfect place for neighborhood ball hockey games. Dryden began playing goalie because he wanted to be like his older brother, Dave.

Dave Dryden, six years older than Ken, moved on to a professional career. Ken was not sure he could make it to the NHL, but things became more promising when he excelled as a college goaltender at Cornell University. Ken Dryden went on to win an NCAA championship at Cornell in 1967. Even then, he enrolled in law school with little thought of playing in the NHL. But the Montreal Canadiens had other plans.

On March 20, 1971, at the Montreal Forum, Ken and Dave Dryden became the first brothers to play goaltender against each other in an NHL game. Both Drydens came on in relief of the starter. Montreal beat Buffalo, 5–2. When the game ended, the two Drydens shook hands at center ice.

Dave Dryden never became more than a backup goaltender, but Ken's career took off. As a rookie, he led the Canadiens to the Stanley Cup championship. He was only getting started. Jacques Plante is the only other goaltender who can match Dryden's six Stanley Cup championships. Dryden was part of the Canadiens' run of four straight Stanley Cups from 1976 to 1979. He earned the Vezina Trophy for allowing the fewest goals against for the season in each of those championship years.

Dryden played only eight NHL seasons. But when he retired, it was clear he had done enough to deserve a place in the Hockey Hall of Fame. Dryden could have continued to play for many more years, but his heart wasn't in it.

"I have always played hockey because I like to play, and as true as that was when I was six years old, it is still true today," Dryden said during his final season. "If I continue to play, it could only be for a different reason, and I won't let myself play that way."[1]

Dryden retired with a record of 258–57–74, including 46 shutouts. His .758 winning percentage is the best among all goaltenders with at least 200 victories.

As great as his Montreal career was, Dryden also is remembered for being the winning goaltender when Canada defeated the Soviet Union in a special series of games between the two countries in 1972. The series was tied going into the final game in Moscow. An entire country celebrated when Paul Henderson scored with thirty-four seconds to play, to give Canada a 6–5 victory.

From his days at Cornell, through the end of his NHL career, Dryden was always associated with winners. In the spring of 1997, he took on another challenge. Dryden was named president of the Toronto Maple Leafs. The Maple Leafs believe he knows what it takes to make them a winning team again.

KEN DRYDEN

BORN: August 8, 1947, Hamilton, Ontario, Canada.

PRO: Montreal Canadiens, 1970–1979.

COLLEGE: Cornell University.

HONORS: Conn Smythe Trophy, 1971; Calder Trophy, 1972; Vezina
Trophy, 1973, 1976–1979; Hockey Hall of Fame, 1983.

Keeping his eye on the puck, Ken Dryden watches it sail over the
top of the crossbar.

TONY ESPOSITO

A NUMBER OF SETS OF BROTHERS have played in the NHL. Few, however, enjoyed as much success as Phil and Tony Esposito. Tony followed his older brother into the NHL, then followed him into the Hockey Hall of Fame. While Phil was a great goal scorer with Chicago, Boston, and the New York Rangers, Tony is one of the best goaltenders in the history of the game.

As a young boy, Tony Esposito often was out of bed before the sun came up on the weekend, ready to get in a full day at the rink. He used to stop at his friend Clipper's house to see if Clipper wanted to join him. "[Clipper] told me to go back to bed where I belonged, then slammed his window in my face. So I'd continue on to the rink alone. But Clipper would join me later, and so would Phil and we'd play and play and play until we were exhausted."[1]

Esposito credits those early days with helping him become an NHL star. "I'm mentally tough. If someone isn't mentally tough, hockey's not their game, goaltending isn't a job they should have," he said. "You need to have competition to be any good and I had competition and success at a young age."[2]

There was a time during high school when Esposito considered giving up the game. He stuck with it and earned a scholarship to Michigan Tech. Esposito won a NCAA championship as a sophomore at Michigan Tech. The Montreal Canadiens owned the right to sign Esposito, and the Canadiens brought him in for a look in 1968. Esposito appeared in 13 games for Montreal and got his name on the Stanley Cup, as the Canadiens went on to win the championship.

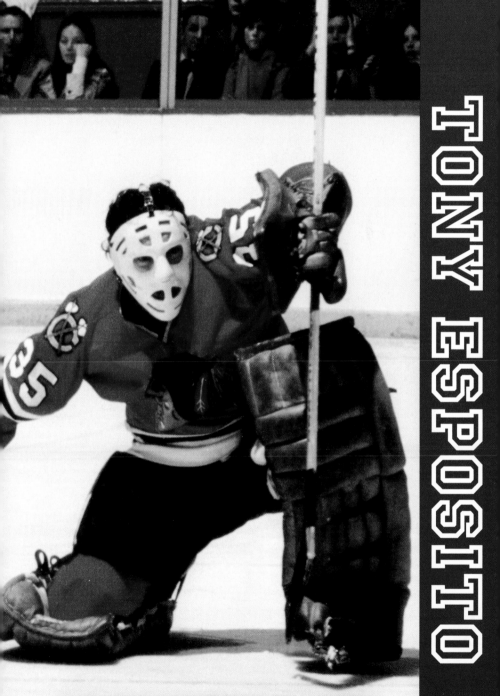

Sliding across the ice, Tony Esposito defends the goal. Esposito was elected to the Hockey Hall of Fame in 1988.

TONY ESPOSITO

Esposito was signed by the Chicago Blackhawks in 1969. There was talk that the Canadiens weren't sure he had what it took to be a top goalie. Esposito had his own style of play. He went down on the ice a lot, and some experts said he "flopped around" too much. Esposito quickly made the Canadiens regret letting him go.

In only his third start as a Blackhawk, Esposito shut out the Canadiens at the Montreal Forum to end their 24-game unbeaten streak at home. He went on to earn 10 shutouts in the first half of the season. He was picked to play in the All-Star Game, where he was a teammate of his brother, Phil.

By season's end, Esposito had posted a remarkable 15 shutouts his first season in Chicago. He was named NHL Rookie of the Year. Blackhawks fans gave him a new nickname, Tony O, and he remained a fan favorite at Chicago Stadium until he retired in 1984.

Playing on a team that included future Hall of Famers Bobby Hull and Stan Mikita, Esposito helped lead the Blackhawks to the Stanley Cup Finals in 1971. The Hawks' opponent? Montreal. Esposito would get another chance to prove his former team wrong.

When the Hawks took a 3–2 lead in the best-of-seven series it looked as if they would win their first Stanley Cup since 1961. But Montreal won Game 6, to set up a showdown at Chicago Stadium in Game 7. The Hawks lost a heartbreaker, 3–2.

Esposito recorded 74 shutouts in his career. He won 30 or more games in eight different seasons. He earned the Vezina Trophy as the NHL's top goaltender three times. Yes, the Montreal Canadiens let a great one get away. They are reminded of this every time they visit Chicago to play the Blackhawks at the United Center. Tony Esposito's No. 35 hangs from the ceiling as one of only four numbers retired by the Blackhawks.

TONY ESPOSITO

BORN: April 23, 1944, Sault Ste. Marie, Ontario, Canada.

PRO: Montreal Canadiens, 1968–1969; Chicago Blackhawks, 1969–1984.

COLLEGE: Michigan Tech.

RECORDS: Recorded 15 shutouts as a rookie in 1969. Had 7 consecutive seasons with 30 or more wins.

HONORS: Calder Trophy, 1970. Vezina Trophy, 1970, 1972, 1974. Hockey Hall of Fame, 1988.

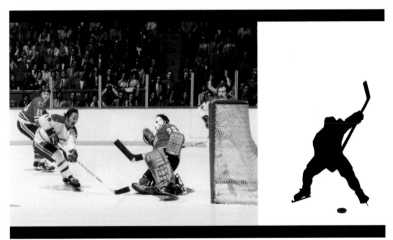

Tony Esposito makes the save, robbing Yvan Cournoyer of the Montreal Canadiens.

GRANT FUHR

THE EDMONTON OILERS OF THE 1980s will be remembered as one of the most explosive offensive teams in NHL history. Led by Wayne Gretzky, Mark Messier, Paul Coffey, and Jari Kurri, the Oilers' firepower was unmatched. As a team, they won four Stanley Cups in five years.

But few teams have won the Cup without a standout goaltender, and the Oilers had theirs in Grant Fuhr. Fuhr was there to erase any mistakes the Oilers made as they pressed the attack. His presence is a major reason that many feel those Oilers teams are the best of all time.

Edmonton won its first Stanley Cup in 1984. The Oilers beat the New York Islanders in the Finals to end the Islanders' string of four consecutive championships. Fuhr sent a message in Game 1 of the Finals that the Oilers weren't all about offense. He shut out the Islanders, 1–0.

Fuhr was a standout throughout the Oilers' championship run. He won the Vezina Trophy as the NHL's best goaltender for the 1987–88 season. The Oilers went on to win their fourth Cup that season.

Fuhr's teammates knew how important he was to their success. Gretzky, for one, considers Fuhr to be the best he has ever seen. "Unlike every other goalie I've ever met, Grant was absolutely unafraid of the puck," Gretzky said.[1] Fear has never been a concern for Fuhr. The proof is in his strong play in the playoffs, when the pressure is on.

Once, when Fuhr was interviewed during the playoffs, he told reporters that the playoffs were his time of year. "This is when I have the most fun. You play eighty-four

GRANT FUHR

Known for his outstanding play in important games, Grant Fuhr helped lead the Edmonton Oilers to four Stanley Cups in the 1980s.

games to get to the playoffs, so you might as well enjoy them when you get here."[2]

By 1990 the Oilers' championship team was being broken up, little by little. Fuhr was traded to Toronto in 1991 in a seven-player deal. It was the beginning of a flurry of moves for Fuhr. Wanting to make room for young goaltender Felix Potvin, the Maple Leafs sent Fuhr to Buffalo in 1992. The Sabres were happy to get a superstar who still was in his prime.

"He's the best goalie I've ever faced, the best I've ever seen, and he's playing better now than he ever has," said former Buffalo center Pat LaFontaine. "I'm glad he's on our side."[3] But Fuhr wasn't a Sabre for long. He was traded to Los Angeles in 1994. Fuhr did not play well as a King, and it looked as though his career might be over.

St. Louis coach and general manager Mike Keenan felt Fuhr could still do the job, so he signed Fuhr as a free agent in 1995. Fuhr not only played well in the 1995–96 season, but also set an NHL record by appearing in 79 games. Fuhr credits his conditioning coach, Robert Kersee, for helping him get in the best shape of his life. Kersee is the husband and trainer of U.S. Olympic track star Jackie Joyner-Kersee.

Fuhr began his sixteenth season in 1996 as the Blues' No. 1 goalie. A six-time All-Star, Fuhr had shown the NHL he still was at the top of his game.

Fuhr was the first black goaltender to play in the NHL and the first black player to get his name on the Stanley Cup. He can be proud of both, as well as of an NHL career that should lead him to the Hockey Hall of Fame.

GRANT FUHR

BORN: September 28, 1962, Spruce Grove, Alberta, Canada.

PRO: Edmonton Oilers, 1981–1991; Toronto Maple Leafs, 1991–1992; Buffalo Sabres, 1992–1994; Los Angeles Kings, 1995; St. Louis Blues, 1995– .

RECORDS: Started 79 games in 1995–1996, an NHL record for goaltenders.

HONORS: Vezina Trophy, 1988.

In a sport traditionally dominated by white athletes, Grant Fuhr was the first black player to have his name carved into the Stanley Cup.

GLENN HALL

Glenn Hall glances behind his net to keep an eye on the opponent.

GLENN HALL

IMAGINE BEING SO GOOD AT DOING something that you are considered one of the best in the world. And at the same time, not being able to enjoy what you were doing. That was life as a goaltender for Hockey Hall of Famer Glenn Hall.

"Playing goal is a winter of misery for me," Hall once admitted during his playing career. "Plenty of times I'm tempted to get into my car and head for home. I'm not knocking the business, because it's given me a high standard of living. On the team plane, when I'd doze off, I'd wake myself up suddenly by kicking out my leg to stop some imaginary shot. . . . By the end of the season I'm tired and fed up. It takes me to July to get over a season."[1]

Hall played eighteen NHL seasons with Detroit, Chicago, and St. Louis. Along with his great success, Hall also is famous for getting sick to his stomach before every game he played in. The thought of having to go out and face pucks being shot at him at nearly 100 miles per hour was almost too much for Hall to stand. "Before a game I keep to myself," Hall said, "because I'm so miserable that I don't think anyone would want me around."[2]

But it never stopped Hall from playing, and playing well. Hall holds an NHL record that will be hard for anyone to break. From the start of the 1955–56 season to early in the 1962–63 season, Hall started and completed 502 consecutive games. His streak was snapped in the twelfth game of the 1962 season, when he was forced to leave a game against Boston in the first period due to a back injury.

Hall's numbers rank him among the game's very best goaltenders. His 84 career shutouts ranks third all-time. He was an 11-time All-Star and won the Vezina Trophy as the league's best goalie three times. His nickname says it all: Mr. Goalie.

Hall's NHL career began in 1954, when Detroit traded its top goalie, Terry Sawchuk, to Boston to make room for Hall. Hall played in all 70 of Detroit's games in 1955. His 2.11 goals-against average and 11 shutouts earned him the Calder Trophy as the NHL Rookie of the Year.

But in 1957, Hall was traded to Chicago. It proved to be one of the best trades the Blackhawks ever made. It was in Chicago that Hall put together his record-setting consecutive games streak. By 1966 Hall decided his nerves couldn't take much more, but when he couldn't find a decent job away from hockey, he returned to the Blackhawks. He went on to share the Vezina Trophy with backup goalie Denis DeJordy.

With 1967 came NHL expansion. Hall was thirty-six years old, so the Hawks decided to protect DeJordy in the expansion draft. Hall was claimed by St. Louis. He was talked out of retiring when the Blues signed him for $47,500, the largest contract ever signed by a goaltender at that time.

The Blues made it all the way to the Stanley Cup Finals that season. Montreal won the Stanley Cup, but Hall did all he could to keep the Blues in every game. Hall earned the Conn Smythe trophy as the playoffs' MVP.

The following year the Blues added another goaltending legend, Jacques Plante, who came out of retirement. Together Hall and Plante combined for 13 shutouts and a 2.07 goals-against average. Backed by their veteran goaltenders, the Blues won the Western Division.

Hall played five seasons with the Blues, then retired in 1971 at the age of forty-three. He went on to a career as a goaltending coach with the Calgary Flames. As painful as his playing days had been, Hall decided to stay a part of the game he loved. Playing hockey gave Hall his share of pain, but also some memories to last a lifetime.

GLENN HALL

BORN: October 3, 1931, Humboldt, Saskatchewan, Canada.

PRO: Detroit Red Wings, 1954–1957; Chicago Blackhawks,
    1957–1967; St. Louis Blues, 1967–1971.

HONORS: Calder Trophy, 1956; Vezina Trophy, 1963, 1967, 1969;
    Conn Smythe Trophy, 1968; Hockey Hall of Fame, 1975.

His body fully extended, Glenn Hall attempts to block the area near
the goal post in case of a wraparound shot.

JACQUES PLANTE

JACQUES PLANTE MADE HISTORY during his days as a goaltender for the Montreal Canadiens. Plante was also known for the changes he made to the game. He was the first goaltender to make the face mask a regular part of his equipment. Others had tried masks, but they felt they couldn't see well enough.

Plante made the decision to wear a mask in games after getting hit in the face in practice by a shot from the powerful Boom Boom Geoffrion in 1954. Plante was wearing a mask and escaped without injury. He would never play without a mask again.

Plante began his hockey career in Quebec, Canada, as a defenseman. He borrowed a pair of his dad's skates to play. Because the skates were too big, Plante knitted some socks for himself to help his feet fill the skates.

Plante put his experience as a defenseman to use as a goalie. Because he was a good skater, Plante decided he would go out and play the puck instead of standing and watching his defensemen do all the work. In time, most goalies would adopt his style. But at the time he received some criticism.

"Before a goalie leaves his net, he has to carefully weigh the situation," Plante said. "Can I get to the puck first or will my opponent? If the chance is good that I'll win, then I take the chance."[1]

Plante was thrown into a tough situation as a Montreal Canadiens rookie during the 1952–53 playoffs. An injury to Montreal's top goalie, Gerry McNeil, forced Plante into action against Chicago. Although he was extremely nervous,

JACQUES PLANTE

Though he is shown here without his mask, Jacques Plante was the first goalie to make it a regular part of his equipment.

Plante shut out the Blackhawks, as the Canadiens won, 3–0. Montreal went on to lose to Boston in the Stanley Cup Finals, but Plante had proven that he was an NHL goaltender.

Plante led the NHL in goals-against average for five straight years during the 1950s. His success carried over into the next decade. Plante won the Hart Trophy as the league's Most Valuable Player in 1962. Only one other goalie, Dominik Hasek, has won the award in the last thirty-five years.

But the Canadiens slumped to third place in 1963. They decided to send Plante to the New York Rangers for goaltender Gump Worsley in a trade that included five other players. Plante spent two seasons in New York, but he decided to retire at the age of thirty-six. His wife had been ill, and his family had stayed in Montreal after the trade.

Plante's retirement ended three years later when he agreed to join the St. Louis Blues in 1968. The Blues had been added to the NHL as an expansion team at the start of the 1967–68 season. They convinced Plante to join veteran Glenn Hall and split the goaltending duties. The forty-year-old Plante had stayed in shape by playing club hockey in Montreal. He proved as much in St. Louis.

In 1968–69, Plante contributed five shutouts and a goals-against average of 1.96, as he and Hall combined to allow the fewest goals for the season. Montreal beat the Blues in the Stanley Cup Finals for the second straight year, but Plante added three playoff shutouts to his remarkable season.

"I don't think I ever played better than I did with St. Louis," Plante said years later.[2]

Plante's name appears 6 times on the Stanley Cup. His 14 playoff shutouts are second only to Clint Benedict's 15. No one can match his 7 Vezina Trophies, awarded each year to the best goalie in the NHL. Plante clearly was one of the very best to ever play the game.

JACQUES PLANTE

BORN: January, 17, 1929, Mont Carmel, Quebec, Canada.

PRO: Montreal Canadiens, 1952–1963; New York Rangers, 1963–1965; St. Louis Blues, 1968–1970; Toronto Maple Leafs, 1970–1972; Boston Bruins, 1972–1973.

RECORDS: Won 40 or more games in a season three times, an NHL record.

HONORS: Vezina Trophy, 1956–1960, 1962, 1969; Hart Trophy, 1962; Hockey Hall of Fame, 1978.

Known as Jacques the Roamer, Plante would often leave the goal crease to play the puck away from the opposing team.

PATRICK ROY

Patrick Roy started his career with the Montreal Canadiens, and led them to two Stanley Cup championships.

IT'S OFTEN SAID OF GREAT PLAYERS that they make those around them better. Their hard work and dedication makes others push themselves further. In the case of Colorado Avalanche goaltender Patrick Roy, his influence goes beyond just his teammates.

"Patrick Roy is a superstar in Quebec," says Francois Allaire, the Canadiens goaltending coach when Roy was with the team. "So now all the good athletes in Quebec want to be goaltenders. Ten years ago in the hockey school, if you couldn't skate you were the goalie. Now the best athletes on the team, they want to play goal."[1]

Growing up in Quebec City, Roy was first attracted to the goaltender position by the look of the goalie pads. Too young to own real equipment, Roy copied the look by strapping pillows to each leg with a belt. One of Roy's prize possessions as a boy was the goalie stick that Quebec Nordiques goaltender Daniel Bouchard gave to him at a public appearance. Bouchard was Roy's hockey hero, and Roy put the stick in his bed every night when he went to sleep.

After an outstanding career in junior hockey, Roy was selected by Montreal in the fourth round of the 1984 NHL draft. He made his NHL debut in 1984 and was the Canadiens' No. 1 goalie by the following season.

Roy considers a nine-minute stretch of hockey in a 1986 playoff game against the New York Rangers the best goaltending he has ever done. Roy made 13 saves in those nine minutes, before Claude Lemieux won the game for the Canadiens at 9:41 of overtime.

The Canadiens went on to win the Stanley Cup that

season. Roy posted a goals-against average of 1.92 in 20 playoff games and was awarded the Conn Smythe Trophy as the Most Valuable Player of the playoffs.

Roy won his second Stanley Cup in 1993. It appeared that he would play his entire career in Montreal, breaking team records along the way, but it wasn't meant to be. Early in the 1995 season, Roy and the Canadiens suffered a one-sided loss to Detroit. Roy was so upset with coach Mario Tremblay for leaving him in for nine goals that he skated off the ice and immediately asked to be traded.

The Canadiens granted his wish when they traded Roy to Colorado. The Avalanche felt Roy was the addition that could bring them a Stanley Cup. They were right. Colorado swept Florida in four games, winning the 1996 Stanley Cup Finals. Roy picked up all 4 wins, including a 1–0 shutout in Game 4. Roy stopped 63 Panthers shots as the Avalanche won in triple overtime.

Roy had never been better. The Avalanche won the Stanley Cup in their first year of existence. They moved to Colorado from Quebec, leaving the team name Nordiques behind. The entire city of Denver seemed to have found a new group of heroes.

Like many professional athletes, Roy is superstitious. He won't skate over a blue or red line. He steps over them as he skates to and from the net. Before every game, he writes the names of his three kids on his stick. Right before the start of each game, Roy turns around in the crease and takes a long look at the net. In his mind he pictures the net getting smaller. Roy also talks to the posts, asking them to help him keep the puck out of the net.

Whatever Roy is doing, it's working. If his career continues on track, he will retire as one of the most successful goaltenders in NHL history.

PATRICK ROY

BORN: October 5, 1965, Quebec City, Quebec, Canada.

PRO: Montreal Canadiens, 1984–1995; Colorado Avalanche, 1995– .

RECORDS: Holds NHL record for most playoff wins in a career.

HONORS: Conn Smythe Trophy, 1986, 1993; Vezina Trophy, 1987, 1990, 1992.

Roy was traded to the Colorado Avalanche early in the 1995–96 season, and helped lead them to victory in the Stanley Cup Finals.

TERRY SAWCHUK

Terry Sawchuk is the NHL's all-time leader in wins and shutouts, as well as games played by a goalie.

TERRY SAWCHUK

THE NUMBERS, AS WELL AS MANY who saw him play, say that Terry Sawchuk is the best goaltender to ever play the game. Major health problems throughout his life have made it a wonder that he was ever able to play at all. Sawchuk played in 971 NHL games, a record among goaltenders. His 447 wins are the most recorded by an NHL goaltender. Sawchuk also is the all-time shutout leader, with 103.

Sawchuk's health problems began when he injured his arm playing football as a child. He was afraid to tell his parents he had been playing football. As a result, his arm didn't heal properly, and his right arm ended up shorter than the other. Prior to reaching the NHL, Sawchuk suffered a serious eye injury when he was cut by a skate.

The injuries continued throughout Sawchuk's NHL career. He needed more than four hundred stitches in his face because of cuts from pucks and sticks. He also broke his shoulder and a number of his fingers. For years he walked with a stoop, because a back injury prevented him from standing straight.

Sawchuk played twenty-one seasons with Detroit, Boston, Toronto, Los Angeles, and the New York Rangers. He was named to 7 All-Star teams and won the Vezina Trophy for fewest goals allowed in a season 4 times.

Sawchuk was signed out of Winnipeg, Manitoba, Canada, by the Detroit Red Wings when he was only sixteen years old. After spending time in the minors, he began his NHL career in Detroit in 1950. He was named Rookie of the Year after posting a 1.98 goals-against average, with 11 shutouts.

Sawchuk was an all-star for each of his first five seasons

with the Red Wings. Detroit won the Stanley Cup in 1952. In eight playoff games, Sawchuk had 4 shutouts and a goals-against average of 0.62.

Then Detroit surprised a lot of people by trading Sawchuk to Boston. The Red Wings decided to make room for Glenn Hall, a young goaltender in their system.

Sawchuk never felt comfortable in Boston. He retired in 1957, during his second season with the Bruins. He complained of always being tired, and it wasn't until a few months later that he found out he was suffering from mononucleosis. By the start of the next season, Sawchuk felt well enough to want to make a comeback. Detroit welcomed him back by acquiring him in a trade for winger John Bucyk, who went on to have a Hall of Fame career as a Bruin.

To make room for Sawchuk, the Red Wings traded Hall to Chicago. Sawchuk played well in his return to the Red Wings, but he was slowed by a painful back injury, eventually undergoing back surgery. At the age of thirty-five he was picked up by Toronto, where he joined forty-year-old goaltender Johnny Bower. The two of them combined to lead the Maple Leafs to the Stanley Cup in 1967. Toronto defeated Montreal in 6 games. The Canadiens outplayed the Leafs overall, but Sawchuk proved to be the difference.

"The win over Montreal had to be the greatest thrill of my career," Sawchuk said. "I had a physical breakdown and a long, difficult recovery period. Many times I wondered if I would ever play hockey again."[1]

Sawchuk was the first goalie to play from a crouch position. Before his time, goalies stood almost straight up. By getting down closer to the ice, Sawchuk felt he could move more quickly and see the puck better. All of the other goalies copied his style. None of them have been able to match his success.

TERRY SAWCHUK

BORN: December 28, 1929, Winnepeg, Manitoba, Canada.

PRO: Detroit Red Wings, 1950–1955, 1958–1964, 1968; Boston Bruins, 1955–1957; Toronto Maple Leafs, 1964–1967; Los Angeles Kings, 1967–1968; New York Rangers, 1968–1970.

RECORDS: Leads NHL with 103 career shutouts; Also holds records for most wins (447) and games played by a goalie (971).

HONORS: Calder Trophy, 1951; Vezina Trophy, 1952, 1953, 1955, 1965; Hockey Hall of Fame, 1971.

Using his catlike reflexes, Terry Sawchuk kicks the puck away from the Maple Leafs' attacker. Sawchuk finished his brilliant career with the New York Rangers.

BILLY SMITH

HOCKEY FANS AREN'T GOING TO FIND former New York Islanders goalie Billy Smith's name among the all-time leaders in many categories. But he's right there in the one category that means the most: Stanley Cup championships. Smith won four consecutive Stanley Cups with the Islanders in a career that ended in 1989, after eighteen seasons.

Smith won 88 playoff games in his career, second only to Patrick Roy. Smith always played his best hockey during playoff time. But whether it was the first game of the season or the seventh game of the Stanley Cup Finals, Smith was always a fierce competitor. Opposing players found out right away that it was not a good idea to get too close to the crease when Smith was in goal. With a swat of his stick, Smith laid down the law in his own way.

"I was the first guy who wouldn't be intimidated," Smith said of his aggressive style. "I got fed up with guys running over the top of me. I loved to stir things up, and if I hadn't done it I probably wouldn't have stayed in the NHL."[1]

The Islanders began their string of championships in 1980. As the Islanders turned into a dynasty behind the play of superstars Mike Bossy, Bryan Trottier, and Denis Potvin, Smith did his share in goal. He won the Vezina Trophy as the NHL's top goaltender in 1982. In 1983, he combined with Roland Melanson to win the Jennings Trophy for allowing the fewest goals against in a season.

To earn championship number four in 1983, the Islanders had to get past a young and talented Edmonton Oilers team in the Finals. The Oilers were led by Wayne Gretzky, who was reminded in Game 1 what Smith was all about.

BILLY SMITH

Billy Smith was the Islanders' netminder for their run of four consecutive Stanley Cup wins, spanning the years 1980–83.

"Billy Smith slashed me on the thigh so bad that I had to leave the game in the third period," Gretzky said. "Billy doesn't like anybody near the crease. In Game 3, Smith used his stick for other purposes, like to block every shot we tried."[2]

The Islanders swept the Oilers in four games to win the Stanley Cup. Smith "was so fantastic they gave him the Conn Smythe Trophy as the Most Valuable Player, and they should have given him two," Gretzky said. "We hated Billy Smith and totally respected him at the same time."[3]

When asked to pick an All-Star team of players he played with and against in his career, Gretzky picked former teammate Grant Fuhr as his top goalie and Smith to his second all-time team.

Smith also is the first NHL goaltender to be credited with scoring a goal. It happened on November 28, 1979, in a game against the Colorado Rockies. The Rockies had pulled their goalie for an extra skater during a delayed penalty against the Islanders. Colorado defenseman Rob Ramage had the puck deep in New York territory. He passed the puck back to the point, but missed connecting with a teammate. The puck slid the length of the ice into the empty Colorado net. Because Smith was the last Islander to touch the puck, he was credited with the goal.

It took eight years for another goalie to score a goal. This time, Philadelphia's Ron Hextall shot the puck into an empty net after Boston had pulled its goalie late in a game.

Smith was known for using his stick on opponents who came too close to the crease. Goaltenders are always looking for any advantage they can get. No one ever claimed that Smith was the best athlete to play goaltender, or the one who had the best technique. Smith simply did everything he could to win, and more often than not he was successful.

BILLY SMITH

BORN: December 12, 1950, Perth, Ontario, Canada.

PRO: Los Angeles Kings, 1971–1972; New York Islanders, 1972–1989.

RECORDS: Credited with first goal ever scored by a goalie, 1979.

HONORS: Vezina Trophy, 1982. Conn Smythe Trophy, 1983. Hockey Hall of Fame, 1993.

Following the puck with his eyes, Billy Smith is ready for the next shot. The Islanders have retired Smith's No. 31.

CHAPTER NOTES

Introduction

1. Richard Beddoes, Stan Fischler, and Ira Gitler, *Hockey: The World's Fastest Sport* (New York: Macmillan Publishing Co., 1974), p. 233.

2. E. M. Swift, "Seems Like Old Times," *Sports Illustrated*, February 20, 1995, p. 64.

3. Ken Dryden, *The Game: A Thoughtful and Provocative Look at Life in Hockey* (New York: Times Books, 1980), p. 119.

4. Swift, p. 66.

Ed Belfour

1. Mike Kiley, "Belfour Looking for Respect," *Chicago Tribune*, December 16, 1992, p. 3.

Martin Brodeur

1. E. M. Swift, "Seems Like Old Times," *Sports Illustrated*, February 20, 1995, p. 61.

2. Stan Fischler, *NHL Goalies* (Toronto: Warwick Publishing, 1994), p. 111.

Ken Dryden

1. Ken Dryden, *The Game: A Thoughtful and Provocative Look at Life in Hockey* (New York: Times Books, 1980), pp. 14–15.

Tony Esposito

1. Tony and Phil Esposito with Tim Moriarty, *The Brothers Esposito* (New York: Hawthorn Books, 1971), p. 17.

2. Mike Kiley, "Hawks Honor Legends," *Chicago Tribune*, November 18, 1988, p. 6.

Grant Fuhr

1. Wayne Gretzky with Rick Reilly, *Gretzky: An Autobiography* (New York: HarperCollins, 1990), p. 60.

2. Jon Scher, "Twin Peaks," *Sports Illustrated*, May 2, 1993, p. 31.

3. Ibid.

Glenn Hall

1. Frank Orr, *Hockey's Greatest Stars* (New York: G. P. Putnam's Sons, 1970), p. 205.

2. Ibid., p. 207.

Jacques Plante

1. Frank Orr, *Hockey's Greatest Stars* (New York: G. P. Putnam's Sons, 1970), p. 123.

2. Ibid., p. 126.

Patrick Roy

1. E. M. Swift, "Seems Like Old Times," *Sports Illustrated*, February 20, 1995, p. 64.

Terry Sawchuk

1. Frank Orr, *Hockey's Greatest Stars* (New York: G. P. Putnam's Sons, 1970), pp. 77–78.

Billy Smith

1. Robin Finn, "Smith Retires, Will Coach Goalies," *The New York Times*, June 6, 1989, pp. A27–28.

2. Wayne Gretzky with Rick Reilly, *Gretzky: An Autobiography* (New York: HarperCollins, 1990), p. 68.

3. Ibid., pp. 68–69.

INDEX